BETWEEN

Husbands & Wives

Edited by **Lois L. Kaufman**

Design by
Michel Design

PETER PAUPER PRESS, INC.
WHITE PLAINS · NEW YORK

For My Ideal Spouse, Bill

Jacket photograph is Currier & Ives's
The Lovers' Reconcilliation, reproduced by permission of
the Museum of the City of New York, 56.300.1256,
from the Harry T. Peters Collection.

≈ CONTENTS ≈

*Ever since Eve gave Adam the apple,
there has been a misunderstanding
between the sexes about gifts.*

NAN ROBERTSON

EXCERPTS FROM THE DIARY OF ADAM AND EVE

by Mark Twain

PART I — EXTRACTS FROM ADAM'S DIARY

Monday . . . We? Where did I get that word? — I remember now — the new creature uses it.

Tuesday . . . The new creature names everything that comes along, before I can get in a protest. And always that same pretext is offered — it *looks* like the thing. There is the dodo, for instance. Says the moment one looks at it one sees at a glance that "it looks like a dodo." . . .

Wednesday Built me a shelter against the rain, but could not have it to myself in peace. The new creature intruded. When I tried to put it out it shed water out of the holes it looks with, and wiped it away with the back of its paws, and made a noise such as some

5

of the other animals make when they are in distress. I wish it would not talk; it is always talking. . . .

Friday The naming goes recklessly on, in spite of anything I can do. I had a very good name for the estate, and it was musical and pretty—GARDEN OF EDEN. . . . The new creature says it is all woods and rocks and scenery, and therefore has no resemblance to a garden. Says it *looks* like a park, and does not look like anything *but* a park. Consequently, without consulting me, it has been new-named—NIAGARA FALLS PARK. . . . And already there is a sign up:

KEEP OFF
THE GRASS

Saturday The new creature eats too much fruit. We are going to run short, most likely. "We" again—that is *its* word; mine, too, now, from hearing it so much. . . .

Sunday Pulled through. . . .

Monday The new creature says its name is Eve. . . . Says it is to call it by, when I want it to come. . . .

Tuesday She has littered the whole estate with execrable names and offensive signs:

THIS WAY TO THE WHIRLPOOL
THIS WAY TO GOAT ISLAND
CAVE OF THE WINDS THIS WAY

She says this park would make a tidy summer resort if there was any custom for it. Summer resort—another invention of hers—just words, without any meaning. What is a summer resort? But it is best not to ask her, she has such a rage for explaining.

Friday She has taken to beseeching me to stop going over the Falls. . . .

I went over the Falls in a barrel—not satisfactory to her. Went over in a tub—still not satisfactory. Swam the Whirlpool and the Rapids in a fig-leaf suit. It got much damaged. Hence, tedious complaints about my extravagance. I am too much hampered here. What I need is change of scene.

Saturday I escaped last Tuesday night, and traveled two days, and built me another shelter in a secluded place, and obliterated my tracks as well as I could, but she hunted me out by means of a beast which she has tamed and calls a wolf, and came making that pitiful noise again, and shedding that water out of the places she looks with. I was obliged to return with her, but will presently emigrate again when occasion offers. . . .

Sunday Pulled through.

Monday I believe I see what the week is for: it is to give time to rest up from the weariness of Sunday. It seems a good idea. . . .

Tuesday She told me she was made out of a rib taken from my body. This is at least doubtful, if not more than that. I have not missed any rib. . . .

Saturday She fell in the pond yesterday when she was looking at herself in it, which she is always doing. . . .

Sunday Pulled through.

Tuesday She has taken up with a snake now. The other animals are glad, for she was always experimenting with them and bothering them; and I am glad because the snake talks, and this enables me to get a rest.

Friday She says the snake advises her to try the fruit of that tree, and says the result will be a great and fine and noble education. . . . I advised her to keep away from the tree. She said she wouldn't. I foresee trouble. Will emigrate.

Wednesday . . . I escaped last night, and rode a horse all night as fast as he could go, hoping to get clear out of the Park and hide in some other country before the trouble should begin; but it was not to be. . . . [I]n one moment the plain was a frantic commotion and every beast was destroying its neighbor. I knew what it meant — Eve had eaten that fruit, and death was come into the world. . . . I found this place, outside the Park, and was fairly comfortable for a few days, but she has found me out. Found me out, and has named the place Tonawanda — says it *looks* like that. In fact I was not sorry she came, for there are but meager pickings here, and she brought some of those apples. I was obliged to eat them, I was so hungry. It was against my principles, but I find that principles have no real force except when one is well fed. . . . She came curtained in boughs and bunches of leaves, and when I asked her what she meant by such nonsense, and snatched them away and threw them down, she tittered and blushed. I had never seen a person titter and blush before, and to me it seemed unbecoming and idiotic. She said I would soon know how it was myself. This was correct. Hungry as I was, I laid down the apple half-eaten — certainly the best one I ever saw, considering the lateness of the season — and arrayed myself in the discarded boughs and branches, and then spoke to her with some severity and ordered her to go and get some more and not make such a spectacle of herself. She did it, and after this we crept down to where the wild-beast battle had been, and collected some skins, and I made her patch together a couple of suits proper for public occasions. They are uncomfortable, it is true, but stylish, and that is the main point about clothes. . . . I find she is a good deal of a companion. I see I should be lonesome and depressed without her, now that I have lost my property. Another thing, she says it is ordered that we work for our living hereafter. She will be useful. I will superintend.

Ten Days Later She accuses *me* of being the cause of our disaster! . . .

Next Year We have named it Cain. She caught it while I was up country trapping on the North Shore of the Erie . . . It resembles us in some ways, and may be a relation. . . . I still think it is a fish . . . The coming of the creature seems to have changed her whole nature and made her unreasonable about experiments. She thinks more of it than she does of any of the other animals, but is not able to explain why. . . .

Sunday She doesn't work, Sundays, but lies around all tired out, and likes to have the fish wallow over her . . . I have come to like Sunday myself. Superintending all the week tires a body so. . . .

Wednesday It isn't a fish. I cannot quite make out what it is. It makes curious devilish

10

noises when not satisfied, and says "goo-goo" when it is. . . . I said I believed it was an enigma; but she only admired the word without understanding it. In my judgment it is either an enigma or some kind of a bug. . . .

Three Months Later . . . It has ceased from lying around, and goes about on its four legs now. . . . As I discovered it, I have felt justified in securing the credit of the discovery by attaching my name to it, and hence have called it *Kangaroorum Adamiensis* . . . It must have been a young one when it came, for it has grown exceedingly since. It must be five times as big, now, as it was then, and when discontented it is able to make from twenty-two to thirty-eight times the noise it made at first. . . . She reconciles it by persuasion, and by giving it things which she had previously told me she wouldn't give it. . . .

Three Months Later The Kangaroo still continues to grow, which is very strange and perplexing. . . . I pity the poor noisy little animal, but there is nothing I can do to make it happy. If I could tame it — but that is out of the question; the more I try the worse I seem to make it. It grieves me to the heart to see it in its little storms of sorrow and passion. I wanted to let it go, but she wouldn't hear of it. . . .

Five Months Later It is not a kangaroo.... It is probably some kind of a bear; and yet it has no tail—as yet—and no fur, except on its head. It still keeps on growing . . . I have offered to get her a kangaroo if she would let this one go, but it did no good . . .

A Fortnight Later I examined its mouth. There is no danger yet: it has only one tooth. It has no tail yet. It makes more noise now than it ever did before—and mainly at night. I have moved out.

Four Months Later I have been off hunting and fishing a month . . . Meantime the bear has learned to paddle around all by itself on its hind legs, and says "poppa" and "momma." It is certainly a new species. . . . I will go off on a far expedition among the forests of the north and make an exhaustive search. There must certainly be another one somewhere, and this one will be less dangerous when it has company of its own species. . . .

Three Months Later It has been a weary, weary hunt, yet I have had no success. In the mean time, without stirring from the home estate, she has caught another one! I never saw such luck. . . .

Next Day I have been comparing the new one with the old one, and it is perfectly plain that they are the same breed. . . . The old one

12

is tamer than it was . . . The new one is as ugly now as the old one was at first . . . She calls it Abel.

Ten Years Later They are *boys;* we found it out long ago. . . . There are some girls now. Abel is a good boy, but if Cain had stayed a bear it would have improved him. After all these years, I see that I was mistaken about Eve in the beginning; it is better to live outside the Garden with her than inside it without her. At first I thought she talked too much; but now I should be sorry to have that voice fall silent and pass out of my life. Blessed be the chestnut that brought us near together and taught me to know the goodness of her heart and the sweetness of her spirit!

PART II — EVE'S DIARY

Saturday I am almost a whole day old, now. I arrived yesterday. . . . I feel like an experiment, I feel exactly like an experiment . . .

Is my position assured, or do I have to watch it and take care of it? The latter, perhaps. Some instinct tells me that eternal vigilance is the price of supremacy. (That is a good phrase, I think, for one so young.)

Everything looks better to-day than it

did yesterday. . . . There are too many stars in some places and not enough in others, but that can be remedied presently, no doubt. . . .

I already begin to realize that the core and center of my nature is love of the beautiful . . . I do love moons, they are so pretty and so romantic. I wish we had five or six; I would never go to bed; I should never get tired lying on the moss-bank and looking up at them.

Stars are good, too. I wish I could get some to put in my hair. . . . When they first showed, last night, I tried to knock some down with a pole, but it didn't reach, which astonished me . . .

So I cried a little, which was natural, I suppose, for one of my age . . .

I followed the other Experiment around, yesterday afternoon, at a distance, to see what it might be for, if I could. But I was not able to make out. I think it is a man. I had never seen a man, but it looked like one, and I feel sure that that is what it is. I realize that I feel more curiosity about it than about any of the other reptiles. If it is a reptile, and I suppose it is; for it has frowsy hair and blue eyes, and looks like a reptile. It has no hips; it tapers like a carrot; when it stands, it spreads itself apart like a derrick; so I think it is a reptile, though it may be architecture.

I was afraid of it at first, and started to

run every time it turned around, for I thought it was going to chase me; but by and by I found it was only trying to get away . . . At last it was a good deal worried, and climbed a tree. . . .

Sunday It is up there yet. Resting, apparently. . . . It looks to me like a creature that is more interested in resting than in anything else. It would tire me to rest so much. It tires me just to sit around and watch the tree. I do wonder what it is for; I never see it do anything. . . .

It has low tastes, and is not kind. When I went there yesterday evening in the gloaming it had crept down and was trying to catch the little speckled fishes that play in the pool, and I had to clod it to make it go up the tree again and let them alone. . . . One of the clods took it back of the ear, and it used language. It gave me a thrill, for it was the first time I had ever heard speech, except my own. I did not understand the words, but they seemed expressive.

When I found it could talk I felt a new interest in it, for I love to talk; I talk, all day, and in my sleep, too, and I am very interesting, but if I had another to talk to I could be twice as interesting, and would never stop, if desired. . . .

Well, I will consider it a man and call it he until it turns out to be something else.

Next week Sunday All the week I tagged around after him and tried to get acquainted. I had to do the talking, because he was shy, but I didn't mind it. He seemed pleased to have me around, and I used the sociable "we" a good deal, because it seemed to flatter him to be included.

Wednesday . . . He does not try to avoid me any more, which is a good sign, and shows that he likes to have me with him. . . . During the last day or two I have taken all the work of naming things off his hands, and this has been a great relief to him, for he has not gift in that line, and is evidently very grateful. . . . The minute I set eyes on an animal I know what it is. I don't have to reflect a moment; the right name comes out instantly . . .

When the dodo came along he thought it was a wildcat—I saw it in his eye. . . . "Well, I do declare, if there isn't the dodo!" I explained—without seeming to be explaining—how I knew it for a dodo . . .

Thursday . . . Yesterday he avoided me and seemed to wish I would not talk to him.

Sunday It is pleasant again, now, and I am happy . . .

I tried to get him some of those apples, but I cannot learn to throw straight. . . .

Monday This morning I told him my name, hoping it would interest him. But he did not care for it. It is strange. If he should tell me his name, I would care. . . .

Although he talks so little, he has quite a considerable vocabulary. This morning he used a surprisingly good word. He evidently recognized, himself, that it was a good one, for he worked it in twice afterward, casually. . . .

Tuesday All the morning I was at work improving the estate; and I purposely kept away from him in the hope that he would get lonely and come. But he did not. . . .

He does not care for me, he does not care for flowers, he does not care for the painted sky at eventide—is there anything he does care for, except building shacks to coop himself up in from the good clean rain, and thumping the melons, and sampling the grapes and fingering the fruit on the trees, to see how those properties are coming along? . . .

There were ashes, gray and soft and delicate and pretty—I knew what they were at once. And the embers; I knew the embers, too. I found my apples, and raked them out, and was glad; for I am very young and my appetite is active. But I was disappointed; they were all burst open and spoiled. Spoiled apparently; but it was not so; they were better than raw ones. Fire is beautiful; some day it will be useful, I think.

EXTRACT FROM ADAM'S DIARY

Perhaps I ought to remember that she is very young, a mere girl, and make allowances. . . . I am coming to realize that she is a quite remarkably comely creature — lithe, slender, trim, rounded, shapely, nimble, graceful . . .

When the mighty brontosaurus came striding into camp, she regarded it as an acquisition, I considered it a calamity; that is a good sample of the lack of harmony that prevails in our view of things. . . . She believed it could be tamed by kind treatment and would be a good pet; I said a pet twenty-one feet high and eighty-four feet long would be no proper thing to have about the place . . .

Nothing ever satisfies her but demonstration; untested theories are not in her line, and she won't have them. It is the right spirit, I concede it; it attracts me; I feel the influence of it; if I were with her more I think I should take it up myself. . . .

Friday . . . I *had* to have company — I was made for it, I think — so I made friends with the animals. . . .

I have learned a number of things, and am educated, now . . . It is best to prove things by actual experiment; then you *know;* whereas if you depend on guessing and supposing and conjecturing, you will never get educated. . . .

[W]hen I have found out everything there won't be any more excitements, and I do love excitements so!

After the Fall

. . . The Garden is lost, but I have found *him*, and am content. He loves me as well as he can; I love him with all the strength of my passionate nature, and this, I think, is proper to my youth and sex. . . . I love certain birds because of their song; but I do not love Adam on account of his singing—no, it is not that; the more he sings the more I do not get reconciled to it. Yet I ask him to sing, because I wish to learn to like everything he is interested in. . . .

It is not on account of his gracious and considerate ways and his delicacy that I love him. No, he has lacks in these regards, but he is well enough just so, and is improving.

It is not on account of his industry that I love him—no, it is not that. . . .

It is not on account of his education that I love him—no, it is not that. . . .

It is not on account of his chivalry that I love him—no, it is not that. . . .

Then why is it that I love him? *Merely because he is masculine,* I think. . . .

Yes, I think I love him merely because he is *mine* and is *masculine*. . . . And so I think it is as I first said: that this kind of love is not a product of reasonings and statistics. It just *comes* — none knows whence — and cannot explain itself. . . .

FORTY YEARS LATER

It is my prayer, it is my longing, that we may pass from this life together . . .

But if one of us must go first, it is my prayer that it shall be I; for he is strong, I am weak, I am not so necessary to him as he is to me — life without him would not be life; how could I endure it? . . . I am the first wife; and in the last wife I shall be repeated.

AT EVE'S GRAVE

ADAM: Wheresoever she was, *there* was Eden.

To write a good love-letter, you ought to begin without knowing what you mean to say, and to finish without knowing what you have written.
JEAN JACQUES ROUSSEAU

Benjamin Franklin, Advice to a Young Man on Early Marriage

Dear Sir

. . . The Character you give me of your Bride (as it includes every Qualification that in the married State conduces to mutual Happiness) is an Addition to that Pleasure. Had you consulted me, as a Friend, on the Occasion, Youth on both sides I should not have thought any Objection. Indeed, from the Matches that have fallen under my Observation, I am rather inclined to think, that early ones stand the best Chance for Happiness. The Tempers and Habits of young People are not yet become so stiff and uncomplying, as when more advanced in Life; they form more easily to each other, and hence many Occasions of Disgust are

removed. And if Youth has less of that Prudence, that is necessary to conduct a Family, yet the Parents and elder Friends of young married Persons are generally at hand to afford their Advice, which amply supplies that Defect; and, by early Marriage, Youth is sooner form'd to regular and useful Life; & possibly some of those Accidents, Habits, or Connexions, that might have injur'd either the Constitution, or the Reputation, or both, are thereby happily prevented.

Particular Circumstances of particular Persons may possibly sometimes make it prudent to delay entering into that State; but in general, when Nature has render'd our Bodies fit for it, the Presumption is in Nature's Favour, that she has not judg'd amiss in making us desire it. Late Marriages are often attended, too, with this further Inconvenience, that there is not the same Chance the Parents shall live to see their offspring educated. *"Late children,"* says the Spanish Proverb, *"are early Orphans."* A melancholy Reflection to those, whose Case it may be! With us in America, Marriages are generally in the Morning of Life; our Children are therefore educated and settled in the World by Noon; & thus, our Business being done, we have an Afternoon & Evening of chearful Leisure to ourselves; such as our Friend at present enjoys. By these early Marriages we are blest with more Children; and from the Mode among us, founded in Nature, of every Mother suckling and nursing her own Child, more of them are rais'd. Thence the swift Progress of Population among us, unparallel'd in Europe.

In fine, I am glad you are married, and congratulate you most cordially upon it. You are now more in the way of becoming a useful Citizen; & you have escap'd the unnatural State of Celibacy for Life, the Fate of many here, who never intended it, but who, having too long postponed the Change of the Condition, find at length, that 'tis too late to think of it, and so live all their Lives in a Situation that greatly lessens a Man's Value. An odd Volume of a Set of Books you know is not worth its proportion to the Set, and what think you of the Usefulness of an odd Half of a Pair of Scissors? It cannot well cut anything. It may possibly serve to scrape a Trencher.

Pray make my Compliments and best Wishes acceptable to your Spouse. I am old and heavy and grow a little indolent, or I should ere this have presented them in Person. I shall make but small Use of the old Man's Privilege, that of giving Advice to younger Friends. Treat your Wife always with Respect; it will procure Respect to you, not from her only, but from all that observe it. Never use a slighting Expression to her, even in Jest, for Slights in Jest, after frequent bandyings, are apt to end in angry earnest. Be studious in your Profession, and you will be learned. Be industrious and frugal, and you will be rich. Be sober and temperate, and you will be healthy. Be in general virtuous, and you will be happy. At least, you will, by such Conduct, stand the best Chance for such Consequences. I pray God to bless you both; being ever your affectionate Friend.

Benjamin Franklin, Advice on the Choice of a Mistress, 1745

To my dear Friend:

I know of no Medicine fit to diminish the violent Natural Inclinations you mention; and if I did, I think I should not communicate it to you. Marriage is the proper remedy. It is the most natural state of Man, and therefore the State in which you are most likely to find solid Happiness. Your Reasons against entering into it at Present appear to me not well founded. The circumstantial Advantages you have in View by postponing it, are not only uncertain, but they are small in comparison with that of the Thing itself, the being married and settled. It is the Man and Woman united that makes the compleat human Being. Separate, she wants his Force of Body and Strength of Reason; he, her Softness, Sensibility, and acute Discernment. Together they are more likely to succeed in the World. A single Man has not nearly the Value he would have in the State of Union. He is an incomplete Animal. He resembles the odd Half of a Pair of Scissors. If you get a prudent, healthy Wife, your Industry in your Profession, with her good Economy, will be a Fortune sufficient.

But if you will not take this Counsel and persist in thinking a Commerce with the Sex inevitable, then I repeat my former Advice, that in all your Amours you should prefer old Women to young ones.

You call this a Paradox and demand my Reasons. They are these:

1. Because they have more Knowledge of the World, and their Minds are better stor'd with Observations, their Conversation is more improving, and more lastingly agreeable.

2. Because when Women cease to be handsome they study to be good. To maintain their Influence over Men, they supply the Diminution of Beauty by an Augmentation of Utility. They learn to do a thousand Services small & great, and are the most tender and useful of Friends when you are sick. Thus they continue amiable. And hence there is hardly such a Thing to be

found as an old Woman who is not a good Woman.

3. Because there is no Hazard of Children, which irregularly produc'd may be attended with much Inconvenience.

4. Because through more Experience they are more prudent and discreet in conducting an Intrigue to prevent Suspicion. The Commerce with them is therefore safer with regard to your Reputation. And with regard to theirs, if the Affair should happen to be known, considerate People might be rather inclined to excuse an old Woman, who would kindly take Care of a young Man, form his Manners by her good Counsels, and prevent his ruining his Health & Fortune among mercenary Prostitutes.

5. Because in every Animal that walks upright the Deficiency of the Fluids that fill the Muscles appears first in the highest Part. The Face first grows lank and wrinkled; then the Neck; then the Breast and Arms; the lower Parts continuing to the last as plump as ever: so that covering all above with a Basket, and regarding only what is below the Girdle, it is impossible of two Women to tell an old one from a young one. And as in the Dark all Cats are grey, the Pleasure of Corporal Enjoyment with an old Woman is at least equal, and frequently superior; every Knack being, by Practice, capable of Improvement.

6. Because the Sin is less. The debauching a Virgin may be her Ruin, and make her for Life unhappy.

7. Because the Compunction is less. The having made a young Girl miserable may give you frequent bitter Reflection; none of which can attend the making an old Woman happy.

8th and lastly. They are so grateful!!!

Thus much for my Paradox. But still I advise you to marry directly; being sincerely

 Your Affectionate Friend, B.F.

Napoleon
to
Josephine

November 28, 1796

I have received the express which Berthier had dispatched from Genoa. . . .

. . . It is not my wish that you should alter any of your plans, or decline the parties of pleasure which are offered you. I am not worth the sacrifice . . .

As for me, to love you alone, to make you happy, to do nothing which would contradict your wishes, this is my destiny and the aim of my life. Be happy, do not concern yourself about me; do not interest yourself in the happiness of a man who lives only in your life, who enjoys only your pleasures, your happiness. When I require from you love such as mine, I do wrong . . .

When I sacrifice to you all my desires, all my thoughts, all the moments of my life, I yield to the ascendancy which your charms, your character, your whole being has gained over my wretched heart. I am wrong if nature has not given me attractions to fascinate you; but what I do deserve from Josephine is her esteem, her respect; for I love her alone, and most passionately.

Adieu, adorable wife, adieu my Josephine. Let fate concentrate in my heart all sorrows, and all griefs; but joy be given to my Josephine. Who merits it more than she? When it shall be proved that she can love no more, I will conceal my profound grief, and I will content myself with being useful and of some advantage to her.

I re-open my letter to give you one kiss. Ah! Josephine! Josephine!

Bonaparte

NAPOLEON TO JOSEPHINE

November 6, 1806

I have received your letter in which you show yourself vexed at certain hard things I say about women; it is true that beyond all I hate intriguing women. I am accustomed to good, sweet and conciliatory women; they are the ones I love. If they have spoiled me, it is not my fault; but yours. Besides, you will see that I have been very good to one woman who showed herself sensible and good, Madame d'Hatzfeld, When I showed her the letter of her husband, she said to me, sobbing with profound emotion and ingenuously, "Ah, that is indeed his writing!" When she read it, her tone went to my soul; she made me suffer. I said to her: "Ah! well, Madame, throw that letter into the fire; I shall never now be able to order your husband to be punished!" She burned the letter and seemed to me very happy. Her husband is now freed of anxiety. Had the above meeting occurred two hours later it would have been too late. You see that I love good, ingenuous, and sweet women; but it is because they resemble you.

Adieu, my love; I am well.

Napoleon

Anne Boleyn to Henry VIII

Sir:

. . . [N]ever Prince had wife more loyal in all duty, and in all true affection, than you have ever found in Anne Boleyn. With such name and place I would willingly have contented myself, if God and your Grace's pleasure had so been pleased.

You have chosen me from a low estate to be your Queen and companion, far beyond my desert or desire. If then, you found me worthy of such honor, good your Grace, let not any light fancy, or bad counsel of mine enemies, withdraw your princely favor from me; neither let that stain, that unworthy stain, of a disloyal heart toward your good Grace, even cast so foul a blot on your most dutiful wife and the infant Princess, your daughter. . . . But let me have a lawful trial . . . Yea, let me receive an open trial, for my truth shall fear no open shames. . . .

If ever the name of Anne Boleyn hath been pleasing in your eyes, then let me obtain this request. . . . From my doleful prison in the Tower, this sixth day of May [1536].

Your most loyal and ever faithful wife,
Anne Boleyn

WALTER RALEIGH

in expectation of being executed, 1603

You shall now receive (my dear wife) my last words in these, my last lines. My love I send you, that you may keep it when I am dead, and my counsel, that you may remember it when I am no more. I would not by my will present you with sorrows, dear Bess, let them go to the grave and be buried with me in the dust; and seeing it is not the will of God that ever I shall see you more in this life, bear it patiently and with a heart like thyself. . . . I send you all the thanks my heart can conceive, or my words can express, for your many travails and cares taken for me. . . . I beseech you, for the love you bear me living, do not hide yourself many days . . .

When I am gone, no doubt, you shall be sought for by many, for the world thinks that I was very rich; but take heed of the pretences of men and their affections . . .

. . . I can say no more; time and death call me away.

. . . My true wife, farewell!

Yours that was, but now not my own.

THE IDEAL SPOUSE

Following are the results of what was intended to be a rigorously unscientific survey of men and women, both married and single, on what they would look for in the ideal mate. If you see yourself, we hope you're pleased. If you don't, there's still time to change!

The Ideal Husband

Makes her laugh

Stops at all rest stops

Has a nice body

Loves to cook

Remembers all birthdays and anniversaries

Enjoys shopping for his wife

Is faithful as a dog, but doesn't look like one

Is easygoing

Is dynamic

Has enough hair

Never leaves the seat up

Is passionate

Has money

Gives gifts, not cash

Loves to give back rubs

Doesn't criticize her driving

Doesn't write "dust me" on the furniture

*Doesn't change TV channels more than
once every 5 minutes*

Tolerates her faults

Is supportive

Is sensitive and aware

Notices selectively

Knows how to program the VCR

Forgives and forgets

Makes love, not lists!

The Ideal Wife

Is a good provider

Hates to shop, except for food

36" 24" 36"

Loves to cook

Gives him space

Loves him to death
Is passionate
Loves Monday night football
Is spontaneous
Tells him he's wonderful at least once a day
Has her own tool box
Isn't controlling
Doesn't back-seat drive
Is supportive
Loves to wash his car
Has empathy
Is independently wealthy
Has a job
Has a career
Loves to iron
Doesn't clean house when he's home
Has a sense of humor like his
Doesn't fix blame
Doesn't fall asleep on the couch watching TV
Makes love, not lists!

QUOTATIONS

We were married 58 years, Sadie, my fair Sadie and I. We always held hands; if I let go, she shopped.

> HENNY YOUNGMAN

I do know this: When a man gets the same cold as his wife, he is sicker and suffers more. My husband told me.

> ERMA BOMBECK

The secret to a successful marriage is having two bathrooms.

> BETTE DAVIS

In any case, let's eat breakfast.

> ISAAC BASHEVIS SINGER,
> to his wife, on hearing that he
> had won the Nobel Prize for Literature

Marriage: A legal or religious ceremony by which two persons of the opposite sex solemnly agree to harass and spy on each other for ninety-nine years, or until death do them join.

ELBERT HUBBARD

Men who married in the 1960's waited an average of seven years before having their first affair; their wives waited 18.
. . . For people married in the 1970's or later, a new "itch" has emerged: Men are faithful an average of five years; women only 4-1/2.

GEORGIA WOOD-LEIGH

Sex is a three-letter word which sometimes needs some old-fashioned four-letter words to convey its full meaning: words like help, give, care, love.

SAM LEVENSON

The graveyards are full of women whose houses were so spotless you could eat off the floor. Remember, the second wife always has a maid.

HELOISE CRUSE

Marriage always demands the greatest understanding of the art of insincerity possible between two human beings.

VICKI BAUM

As you get older, I think you need to put your arms around each other more.

BARBARA BUSH

A happy marriage is a long conversation that always seems too short.

ANDRÉ MAUROIS

Make sure you never, never argue at night. You just lose a good night's sleep, and you can't settle anything until morning anyway.

ROSE KENNEDY

A man is in general better pleased when he has a good dinner upon his table than when his wife speaks Greek.

SAMUEL JOHNSON

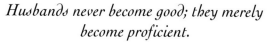

Husbands never become good; they merely become proficient.

H. L. MENCKEN

Real life is in the dishes.

ANNA QUINDLEN

. . . [The] urge for revenge is a fact of marital life.

JANE SMILEY,
Good Will

It can't be so easy being the husband of a "modern" woman. She is everything his mother wasn't—and nothing she was.

MABEL ULRICH

If a married couple puts a penny in a pot for every time they make love in the first year, and takes a penny out every time after that, they'll never get all the pennies out of the pot.

ARMISTEAD MAUPIN

Marriage is our last, best chance to grow up.

JOSEPH BARTH

Alice has always been fond of castles. She likes to imagine someone like the seventeenth Baron of Provolone presiding over the estate while the lady of the house — once just an ordinary girl from some place like Harrison, New York — is waited on by hordes of liveried servants, every one of whom addresses her as Principessa. *As it happens, I always address Alice as* Principessa *myself while we're traveling in Italy; I find it improves the service.*

CALVIN TRILLIN

One can always recognize women who trust their husbands, they look so thoroughly unhappy.

OSCAR WILDE

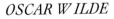

Any married man should forget his mistakes — no use two people remembering the same thing.

DUANE DEWEL

Take my wife . . . please!

HENNY YOUNGMAN

My husband will never chase another woman. He's too fine, too decent, too old.

GRACIE ALLEN

If you want to know how your girl will treat you after marriage, just listen to her talking to her little brother.

SAM LEVENSON

A woman knows there are two sides to every question: there is her husband's side and there is the right side.

ANONYMOUS

It begins with a prince kissing an angel. It ends with a baldheaded man looking across the table at a fat woman.

ANONYMOUS

Marriage is not just spiritual communion and passionate embraces; marriage is also three-meals-a-day and remembering to carry out the trash.

DR. JOYCE BROTHERS

It destroys one's nerves to be amiable every day to the same human being.

BENJAMIN DISRAELI

The reason marriages don't last is because women can't stand it when a man leaves the toilet seat up.

WHOOPI GOLDBERG

I can now appreciate the widow with her young son, while her late lamented husband lay in state in the front of the church, and the minister was doing quite a good job in the eulogistic field. But at a certain point she couldn't take it any longer. Finally she said, "Johnny, you go up and see if that's your pa in that casket."

EVERETT M. DIRKSEN

Fidelity is knowing who you belong to and having the decency to pass up the rest.

ANN LANDERS

I know what I wish Ralph Nader would investigate next. Marriage. It's not safe — it's not safe at all.

JEAN KERR

An ideal husband is one who treats his wife like a new car.

DAN BENNETT

He changed me enormously simply by marrying me. Women marry their husband's lives, not vice versa. Whenever there was a conflict of interests, his prevailed.

CLARE BOOTHE LUCE,
about Henry Luce

Why does a woman work ten years to change a man's habits and then complain that he's not the man she married?

BARBRA STREISAND

When you are old and gray and full of
   sleep,
And nodding by the fire, take down this
   book,
And slowly read, and dream of the soft
   look
Your eyes had once, and of their
   shadows deep;

How many loved your moments of glad
   grace,
And loved your beauty with love false or
   true;
But one man loved the pilgrim soul in
   you,
And loved the sorrows of your changing
   face.

And bending down beside the glowing
   bars
Murmur, a little sadly, how love fled
And paced upon the mountains overhead
And hid his face amid a crowd of stars.

WILLIAM BUTLER YEATS,
When You Are Old

48